CHANGE YOUR DICTIONARY CHANGE YOUR LIFE

Christopher Rivas

This book is for you!

Share it with your friends, family and the world under the terms of Creative Commons Attribution 3.0 License (which means you can share and remix this work, so long as you attribute the Original work to the author)!

"This realization is dedicated to my family, the solid roots I grow from.
& to Nelson Mandela who will forever remind the world that no matter ***what the circumstances*** you can emerge with a smile that could light the heavens, euphoric and radiant"

On The Shoulders Of Giants

I am not an expert, nor am I an enlightened being.

I'm just the guide and the explorer. If you find anything amazing in this book, it's thanks to brilliant minds who acted as resources, critics, contributors, proofreaders, and references. If you find anything ridiculous in this book, it's because I didn't heed their advice.

Though indebted to hundreds of people, I wish to thank a few of them up front, here listed in alphabetical order: Any left unmentioned

Dave Asprey	Affan Arif
Rev. Dr. Michael Beckwith	Leo Babauta
Fu-Ding Cheng	Sean-Loui Dumas
Timothy Ferris	Akuyoe Graham
Nicole Hellendoorn	Sally Hope
Brian Johnson	Ellie King
Josh King	Vishin Lakhiani
Kathryn Kos	Eden Malyn
Ari Meisel	Crisan Morgan
Andrew Mcfarlane	Molly O'Leary
Ido Portal	Eric Rios
Gabriella Rhodeen	Jason Silva
Luke Sniewski	Mark Sisson
Sophia Wang	Amber Zuckswert

DISCLAIMER

I (Christopher Rivas) am not a medical doctor. The opinions expressed in my books, videos, and websites reflect my personal experiences and ongoing investigations into a life worth living; A thriving, vibrant, happy, exciting, healthy, loving, abundant life worth living.

The material in *Change your Dictionary, Change your Life* and many of Lifestyle Dezines complimentary guides is meant to serve as a comprehensive collection of time tested and proven strategies that the author has used and implemented and applies to himself, individuals, andclients. All summaries, tips, tricks, programs, strategies are only recommendations by the author and reading this book does not guarantee that ones results will exactly mirror our own results. Change your Dictionary, Change your Life has made all reasonable efforts to provide current and accurate information for the readers of this book. The authors will not be held liable for any unintentional errors or omissions that may be found.

Whether because of the general evolution of the internet, or the unforeseen changes in company policy and editorial submission guidelines, what is stated as fact at the time of this writing may become outdated or simply inapplicable at alter date. Great effort has been exerted to safeguard the accuracy of this writing. Opinions regarding similar platforms have been formulated as a result of both personal experience, as well as the well-documented experience of others.

No part of this publication shall be reproduced, transmitted, or resold in whole or in part in any form, without the prior written consent of the author.

Who would you be if you *were free?*

If you removed every obstacle in your path?

If you saw beauty everywhere, in everything.

Asked *what's the best possible outcome*, and knew that everywhere you are is serenity, simply because you are.

Who would you be if you knew that nothing would be the same if you did not exist.

If you knew that you are not just here to fill space or to be a background character in someone else's movie.

That you have such power and influence in this world, and a healthier, thriving, happier, and more whole you leads to an improving world.

You can live what should be vs.what is.

You can know the truth.

You can have it all.

Really.

Change Your Dictionary
Change Your Life

Welcome:

"The dictionary is the only place where success comes before work." ~ Vince Lombardi

Out of 7 Billion people today I dance with you. Coincidence? I think not. I understand why you're reading this.

Life is not that deep a concept.
It is the world looked through the eyes of a child.
Lets not postpone it anymore. No more waiting for tomorrow - it never comes -
Live it today.
Let life start caressing you today. Flowing through you today.

"Without you the universe will lose some poetry, some beauty: A song will be missed, a note will be missed, there will be a gap … Nobody has ever told you that. "
~ Osho

Nobody has given you the feeling that you are loved, respected, and that you are needed.

I'm not trying to convert you, rather I'm trying to create rebels who are free, free from the old ways of thinking that no longer serve us; armed with tricks and tools- not simply logic, not simply airy-fairy.

Perfectly evolving so that we can be monks with Ferraris, Buddha's with six packs, and well-fed Brahmin.

I have used these techniques for myself and clients to a hundred percent success, **there is no loss to observing our minds**, to focusing on the words we speak, to realizing who we are. Waking up to *an awareness of* what we say and do matters, a lot; there is only up from here, there is only winning.

I find this work to be the foundation to creating a magical life.

What you say matters. A Lot! You are what you speak.

Your words are a final product of your perception, your thoughts, and the way you view and react to your world- because this is your world.

MY STORY

"The mind is a superb instrument if used rightly. Used wrongly, however, it becomes very destructive." Eckhart Tolle

My name is Christopher Rivas; I'm an actor, artist, writer and the founder of Lifestyle Dezine. A serious lover of life, an epiphany addict, thoroughly obsessed with how magical life is. I was born and raised in the delicious melting pot that is New York City, my flavor – Dominican and Colombian, raised by two parents who were figuring it out on the fly, who showed me what the soul is capable of when it has a mission, when that mission is rooted in love.

I'm a human with doubts and insecurities- it took me a long time to learn to love Christopher Rivas. I was short for so long, I have a big nose, I have big ears, and I was never good enough. These things penetrated my emotions and I started to feel sorry for myself and there was the part inside begging to come out (a whisper, sometimes a yell) saying, "Chris you are perfect just the way you are."
I don't know when or why, but I know when you know, you know, and all of a sudden I was the most beautiful fellow in the world.

Because I finally knew who I was, a spiritual being, here for way more than task and to-do list; and when you find out who you are and that the creator (God, universe, deity, mother/father, nameless) made you to be as you are, and that it's all alright. It takes time.

If you're going to change habits and thought patterns, decide now: I have faith in God and myself that I'm going to start now and know that it takes work.

Everyday is a rich and full practice for me to keep growing and learning, to stay on path with my purpose. Everyday I am grateful to know the things I love so I can give myself to them. Getting here was rough. All that hate for myself had me living a lie. I wasn't happy, I was miserable, no reason why, I just knew there was *more*, this need to be alive sparked me on a downward spiral, chasing the wrong things, trying to find life from outside effects, persuaded by moments of euphoria, afraid of silence, of being alone, addicted to anything that gave me life-if only for a moment. I couldn't imagine happiness, peace that lasted longer than a couple of minutes at a time. I was stealing, I was afraid, I wanted everyone to like me, I was sinking, and I was a pathological liar to others and myself. I created this facade of a life I lived, a false life. Then in a snowball effect, I got caught red handed, caught stealing, I got caught lying, cheating, not trying, I made a fool out of myself in public, my girlfriend left me, my body was in the worst shape it had ever been, and life was more a burden than a joy, all I could think was, "how much worse can it get?" And to top it all off, the thing that hurt the most, my family was furious with me because of my selfish ways. I wasn't the man my parents raised me to be, I wasn't the man I claimed to be and the world saw me for my phoniness. I deceived people I cared about. I lost peoples trust. I was living to be liked, to be cool, to get invited to the parties. I fell so hard, I knew there was more, I wanted more, and how could I let it all get here. There was so much pain, a flood of need, want, envy and all these blessings, so many blessings I just wanted so badly to be grateful for. I cried for hours, I didn't know we could hold that many tears, my soul heart… Finally, I gave up, I stopped fighting, I looked within and I said *"thank you"*, and I meant it, I could finally stop asking, stop blaming others for my unhappiness, and I could start thanking everything for allowing me to be here, in this moment, the only moment possible.

I was thankful for EVERYTHING, I mean everything.

The ugly and the beautiful, these are just words, qualifiers. I could name all my mishaps as ugly or I can claim them as beautiful and necessary moments, that without them, there would be no right now. I was living within this limited perspective that I created, these ideas, traps, words that controlled me; I put myself in a cage of my own fears. In my opinion the violet that breaks the rocks is more beautiful than the roses in a flower shop.

Change your dictionary change your life flooded my brain.

That's what I woke up to. Change from within. Changing how I saw and spoke about the world and my place in it would change the world. I could no longer be a victim to it, but rather I could place myself, have it move for me, around me. All things could be for my growth, my good. I wasn't stuck, I was no longer a victim of circumstance, no one could make me feel what I didn't allow myself to feel, and all the things my soul wanted, needs rooted in love, would start coming to me.

I could watch the rain ruin my day or I could begin to see it through *rain drop lenses*; how it extenuates colors, makes the ordinary vibrant and explosive. I wasn't stuck in the rain on my way home, ruining my shoes; I was dancing in it, thanking it for all it does, for its cleansing properties, (including my shoes), I was celebrating knowing the sun will soon shine –it always does.

If the news (which isn't at all *new*, there is nothing

new about it) made me upset, I didn't need to watch it. If people didn't raise me up, bring me joy, I didn't need to hang out with them, I could choose how to live my life, how to grow, how to learn, how to love.

I began to see the other side. The good in the bad, the joy in the formerly boring. The blessings (everywhere) in abundance!

I began listening, receiving, allowing myself to see things for what they really were. For so long I fought what was, I fought anything I didn't deem as *right*- that's stressful, it's exhausting.

How do we know this moment is the right moment? It's the only moment. Literally, nothing airy-fairy about it, there is no other option. Knowing this we might as well enjoy it, love it, grow from this place, there is no other place.

Suddenly everyone was brilliant, everyone was a genius, and I'm fool if I take it all for granted. There is no me, no now without them- every encounter, every person, every interaction.

My dictionary began to change. *Can't* became *won't*. *Forgiveness* became the real *F word*. *Anger* was one letter away from *Danger*.

Accept-Accept–Accept burst out at me at all times,

everywhere. It's simply smoother this way. More flow.

The three G's: Give- Generosity - Generously

No more accidents, no more *to-do list* (that I sometimes hold onto so tightly they burn), I am now in the practice of allowing things to unfold. There is a plan, whatever you want to call it, the Universes plan, Gods plan, and every other powerful, mythical, 5-arm deity one can believe in. That plan is a life of abundance, abundant love, energy, joy, wealth-here and now. I truly believe this with all my heart.

I now know my being here is not a coincidence, your reading this, my falling, my rising, and our connection or that any meeting is simply a random event cannot be coincidence.

I Challenge You to Look In The Mirror

"The fact that we live at the bottom of a deep gravity well, on the surface of a gas covered planet going around a nuclear fireball 90 million miles away and think this to be normal is obviously some indication of how skewed our perspective tends to be."
— Douglas Adams

I challenge you to watch the words that leave your mouth, pay attention to how you are coloring the world. Are you seeing the good, or stretching out the bad? It'll never go away unless we allow it.

Our habits are what we are. They are hard to break, but we must own them, we must be able to choose those we need and lose the ones that no longer serve us. This is the first obstacle we must overcome before getting to step one – *Accepting the landscape*; We have to accept the landscape as is, we have to love the soil, rich, nutrient, well kept soil, and then begin to cultivate our gardens from that place… **SELF LOVE** ... Are your dietary needs, meditation, exercise, and breathing time selfish? Or is it self-love? Is it time you could be spending getting things done? Or is it the reason you are so effective at getting things done?

Are your 10 minutes of self-love invaluable? I hope so.

We can change our Dictionary; we can determine our very own DEFINITIONS… Their success does not need to be mine. I don't want the red BMW; I want to teach a child a day how to read. Or I do want the red BMW, but I also want to teach a child a day to read and meditate. Whatever it is, if it comes from an authentic place, a place of purpose - by designing our life, our way, we canhave it all to teach a child a day to read and meditate. Whatever it is, if it comes from an authentic place, a place of purpose- by designing our life, our way, we can have it all.

"The soul becomes dyed with the color of its thoughts." - Meditations by Marcus Aurelius

What's The Truth?

"If you tell the truth, you don't have to remember anything." — Mark Twain

Why do some have it all and others don't? They see the world as the observer, they have had a paradigm shift, and they know the truth: That they can control what they see, what they do, what they speak, and most importantly how they act.

"Am I everything I claim to be? Do I practice what I preach? Am I wearing a mask? Do I truly believe the words I speak?" …

We have to ask ourselves:
What kind of world do we want to live in?
What kind of world do we want our children—and their children—to live in?
What is our role or contribution in bringing about this new world?

If you live through defeat, you're not defeated. If you are beaten but acquire wisdom, you have won. Lose yourself to improve yourself. Only when we shed all self-definition do we find who we really are.

When you ask yourself these questions, you live these questions. And you realize that you're not alone but part of a huge impulse in collective consciousness. When you realize this, it energizes you and gives you passion for what you want to create right in this moment.

Are you someone who's willing to stand for the truth and reality of Spirit, of an abundant life where dreams do come true, where dreams are reality in a disbelieving world? Why is it important that we live our beliefs, do not shy away from them, and that we fully dive in? Because when we awaken to that truth and reality, we see much more deeply into the nature of who we really are, into the nature of reality itself, and we discover a fearless courage to live this life for the highest reasons. I think the degree to which each and every one of us is willing to do that is the degree to which we're actually going to have a significant effect.

"Why Don't You Live There Yet?"
Big changes are the results of many tiny little steps. Less is more. Let us do less more often.

A good place to answer this question: **Your home**. Your living space. Your car. Your inbox. These things matter. How they are kept matters. It's not the big things, but rather the little things.
We can't allow our living spaces to fall into disarray.

Our outside world is simply a reflection of our interior selves. The world is our mirror.

When we let little things slide, we send the message to ourselves that our little complaints and discomforts are significant enough to derail life. When we neglect to do such simple things as fold our clothes and keep our eating space clean, simply because we are tired or frustrated or upset, we are saying to ourselves that our emotional ups and downs are so powerful to justify holding up our daily practice. Basically, they are emergencies, what is an emergency but something so important, so dire, that it justifies a break of routine?

And if every small thing is an *emergency* that must be tended to, we will never be able to make forward progress in our lives.
If we are always justifying them, they will always master us. Our lives will be run by our emotional state, rather than by our ideals, principles, and intentions.

We might use every little thing to justify:
- Eating unhealthy
- Staying up late
- Drinking more than we should
- Skipping a workout
- Leaving our homes a mess

But what's the truth??

So, the next time you've had a late night or a rough day at work and you just want to throw your stuff on the floor, ask yourself if the emotional grip is really an emergency, or if you're just giving in to make yourself feel important. Do you really want to lose out on the benefits of a clean/open space (vital for creativity and peace of mind), a healthy meal, or a good night's rest, in exchange for a few minutes of self-importance? Or are you powerful enough to swallow the need for self-indulgence so you can get back to doing work that matters?

Solution:

Change Your Dictionary Change your Life
(A movement of the mind)

I want to teach you how to end your own suffering.
Teach you how to find the magic in all things.
How to be Free, fully free, emotionally, spiritually, mentally, free!
Before you get into this I encourage you to drop it all as if none of it ever happened, shake off everything that no longer serves you - it doesn't mean you don't care, it means you are FREE from History & Time.
The work is a tool to bring Truth into place of the

Stories about what SHOULD be.

Life is a DANCE between what you desire most and fear most.

She wants to be famous vs. She needs to be closer to her children.

Lets **ESCAPE TO REALITY**

Escape TO, not Escape FROM

We live in a world with such oxymorons as "Peace-Keeping-Missiles".

Flip the script.

Anger is one letter away from D[anger].

What could you build that you'd want to escape to instead of escape *from*?
How could you wake up excited … eager … full of energy to make progress on a life that mattered, work that mattered? Not bogged down in your inbox, not distracted by tasks that drain your energy… but genuinely happy about what lay ahead?
If you manage to find or create this extraordinary work, in a world of ordinary routine, better find or create a way to keep it.

You might think that this perspective is a privileged way of life, something available only to those who are rich or successful or otherwise endowed with choices unavailable to you. No, that isn't true. Speaking for myself: There was a time in my life where I remember not seeing my parents, both worked two fulltime jobs, my father was a super from 9pm-5pm, then a door man form 7pm-3am; my mother worked at a doctors office 9pm-5pm and then the overnight at NYU medical. I don't come form privileged stock according to what we call 'privilege' but I do come from love, sacrifice, hustle, great intentions - we all have this in us, from this place al things are possible.

This perspective is a prerequisite to a new way of life. You start with this perspective and then you work toward creating the actual life. It's not simple, it's not easy, and it's not always straightforward. But it's always worth it! It's the whole point! You begin with it and then you carry it forward. When new things come your way, you evaluate them against the standard of escaping. Would I want to do this if I didn't have to? Would I be excited about waking up and working on this?

If yes, great!

If no, that's what you need to escape *from.*

Preparing for Change (not all change is bad)

Let us be honest…. Change is hard… This is difficult work… Don't be fooled and don't be surprised. But there are great rewards on the other side.

This is WHAT HONESTY WILL GET YOU?

#1: PEOPLE MIGHT STOP SPEAKING TO YOU
Forget personal branding. Start to dip your toes into **personal honesty**. Let me tell you what will happen. Your "*friends, family*" might stop speaking to you. I have experienced this not just from myself but all of the people I consider "honest". Some of your friends, some of your colleagues will avoid you, some investors will shun you. Your personal "network" will transform and shift. My own personal motto is: honesty to a point. I will never harm anyone. I believe in what Buddha said to his son Rahula the day after he showed up after abandoning his son for 7 years:
Before, during, and even AFTER you say something, make sure it doesn't hurt anyone.

#2 PEOPLE WILL THINK YOU ARE GOING CRAZY
The next thing that will happen is people will ask, "are you going crazy?" because honesty can be

abrasive, honesty can force others to wake up and that can be threatening, so they will call you mad. Then people might send emails to your friends, "is he as crazy as he sounds?" And that's how I make friends now because introductions will be made and people will have to find out for themselves.

#3 PEOPLE WILL GET FRIGHTENED
So they will call you names. Oh, that guy is just trying to be a "contrarian", for instance. Or an "idiot". Or worse. I've been called everything.
They need to understand why you are telling the truth. Why you are being honest about what you really think. In meetings at the office everyone is quiet. You're not supposed to speak up. But you will.

#4 PEOPLE WILL *gravitate to your charisma*
People will come back to you and gravitate towards you. Because you're entertaining – if 20,000 people are lying and only 1 person is telling the truth then that 1 person is going to stand taller than anyone. At first people will come back to you for voyeuristic reasons. Why? Because they know if they watch Real Housewives they aren't watching anything "Real" and they aren't watching "Housewives". But you're real. So they want to know what you'll do next.

#5 PEOPLE WILL TRUST YOUR ADVICE

People will also come back for advice. Not always because they agree with you. But because they know the advice is coming from the heart and not because there is anything for sale. It's like Google can't cure anything. But they can direct you to all the people who can. So you go back to Google because you might not always find what you want but at least you know they are trying hard to direct you to the right place.

We've all hidden our failures in dark comets orbiting the peripheral edges of the solar system, where the sun is dark and faded. But when someone brings their orbit close to the sun we want to land there for a brief moment and see if actual living conditions exist. And if so, then maybe a small settlement can be formed, advice can be asked, a failure can be related to, a friendship can be formed.

#6 YOU BECOME FREE

At first we hug our boundaries in chains. We think "if we tell the boy/girl we like them, they might not like me back". We think, "If I say I like this candidate, my friends might hate me." If I say X, everyone else might say Y. And so on. But more and more we start to feel where those boundaries are and we push them out. We push them further and further away from ourselves. Until finally they are so far away it's as if they don't exist at all. We create the imprint on the world instead of them creating it on us. You don't need money for that. Or a big house. Or a fancy degree or car. Every day, just push out those boundaries a little further.

We reach for that **freedom**, and eventually, the boundaries are so far away we begin to feel the pleasures of true freedom.

And it feels good. **Real good**.

Change means to become.

Are you ready? Then let's go.

1. ACCEPT THE LANDSCAPE:

Important first step is to recognize the world you live in and the ways it has limited you.

We all just want to be mesmerized, not precise, but effortless, FREE. So walk slow, crick your neck back, and unwind your spine so that you can watch this world inside out. All is not lost in translation, the best relationship I ever had was with someone who didn't speak my "language". Like babies, we spoke God, we made it work.

These are the things we hear when we start listening behind the cracks, and we place ourselves in the underbelly of the world.

Self-blame:

Lets give up the story!
That its not your fault and this did not happen to you, it happened.
If you want to achieve your dreams, you're going to need to take full responsibility for your life. That means no blaming your parents, friends, relatives or bad luck for where you are in life. Recognize that some things are beyond your control, but take

responsibility for the way every situation turns out.

"Spare me for the desire of love, approval or appreciation…I am totally independent of the good or bad opinions of others" - may we live independent of the good or bad opinion of others!

If you think someone else is causing your problem your insane! We must work on our minds.

Stress doesn't come form the facts, it comes from the MEANINGS that we give the facts.

New life comes from new choices, but we have to make conscious choices.

We need to eliminate and liberate ourselves. Less is more. Your life doesn't need to be stressed. You don't need to be busy. There is another way. We will work smarter not harder. I will assist in finding you inefficiencies and eliminate them, so we can liberate ourselves. We will find your strengths and multiply them!

The Truth will set you free but first it might piss you off, we'll see... What the worst that can happen?

Pleasing syndrome:

"I don't know the key to success, but the key to failure is trying to please everyone." — Bill Cosby

The disease to please.

Losing ourselves to meet someone else's needs? Saying "Yes" when you mean "No". Again: A "No" to someone else can be a "Yes" to you.

We are what we put out into the world. The universe wants us to be happy, it benefits from our good energy. So lets allow, and put ourselves in that place so all parties win!

For too long I felt bad about not taking care of my needs? I said yes to parties I didn't want to go too. I hung out when all I wanted to do was be alone. I smiled when I really needed to cry. I lost myself in being there for others.

When being completely honest with myself and the world around me, I lost people who I thought were friends, but they enjoyed this always wonderful facade of me, in my honesty I gained true friends who respected my "no's" and loved unconditionally.

Nothing builds up faster and tears you down quicker than bitterness and resentment.

It's crazy to believe that one can always say yes, crazy to believe one can always be the shoulder to cry on, the soundboard for others. It's a give and take, and we can give so much better when we have received and are in a balanced place.

Do things from a genuine "I want to" standpoint, not out of need, or fear of what they might think and watch how you begin to breathe a little easier.

3 Kinds of Business:

Mine

Yours – - partner, boss, lover

The Beyond/Universe/Spirit (whatever you like) – *earthquake, tornado, weather, traffic.*

There are things you can control There are things you cant control.

Stay in your own business.
We can only change *our* own mind. Everything out there is a misconception of *our* own thinking,
If you keep trying to control others, blame others; you are caught in this dream that you have control. You can control you, nothing else.
Wake up to a new reality, a reality grounded in truth. *What from your thoughts is true? What from your thoughts can you make true?*
The work (meditation, prayer, reading, exercise, diet, lifestyle) is a tool to bring Truth into place of the Stories about what is.
- Lets throw the stories in the trash! Child shouldn't, car shouldn't, spouse shouldn't, and boss shouldn't accept reality. Lets say what is and accept reality.
"Spare me for the desire of love, approval or appreciation". "I am totally independent of the good or bad opinions of others".

May we live independent of the good or bad opinion of others!

Whatever you focus on you are going to find, you are going to feel. Seek and you shall find.
- They don't care mentality, you'll find it!
- Coincidences are everywhere, you'll find them!
- You have a horseshoe in your ass, you'll have it!

2. DEAL WITH TRAPS

Now that you see the landscape clearly, you are ready to set off down the path and avoid the traps that are waiting for you. You have graduated.

Balance:

"So be sure when you step, Step with care and great tact. And remember that life's A Great Balancing Act. And will you succeed? Yes! You will, indeed! (98 and ¾ percent guaranteed) Kid, you'll move mountains." — Dr. Seuss (Oh, The Places You'll Go!)

The most important word in my dictionary.
There is nothing without it.
Many words carry power but the one that encompasses all, and the one that is most important, is **BALANCE**. I find it difficult to come up with another single word that is more crucial to the achievement of a healthy life other than balance. Just think of it… physically, visually, aurally and even orally.
Everything has a right to live. Everything wants to exist and we have to respect that. The weaker side in any relationship naturally demands things, because of the need for mutual balance. War, sickness, unhappiness is imbalance. You can get sick from either over-eating or under-nourishment. Peace, health, happiness, is balance.
This thing called balance, that which we often take for granted, is crucial to the enjoyment of our everyday life. In vision, in sound, in touch, taste, art, music, sports, drama, architecture, food, and-scaping, on land, sea and air, in short, in LIFE, it is absolutely crucial to a pleasant fulfilling experience! Think about your own life. Think about those things that jar you, annoy you, make you uncomfortable, and I'll venture to say that you will find an imbalance at the root of your discomfort. Some of these disturbances can be of short duration, or they can be chronic problems. In our "make-believe theatre" they are man-made and short-lived. In life they are also man-made but they

can have long-lasting dire consequences. * Do not assume that balance is synonymous with equal or *symmetrical.* On the contrary, balance is often complex and un-equal. A perfect example is to look at one of life's exquisite wonders… A Tree. By its nature, a tree, no matter how you look at it, is always in balance. Even after a lightning bolt may sever a major limb, in time it will alter its growth and form, and re-achieve a balance. Isn't that amazing? Would that we could do that with our own lives.

But man is not as simple and deep-rooted as a tree.

During its gnarled, twisted and disfigured transformation, the tree can be exquisitely beautiful. It is nothing short of majestic in its slow, but positive ascent to a restored, balanced life. Nature, in its purest form is lovely and glorious and wonderful.

This is not meant to be a world-paper on balance. It is only my own, simple explanation to make you aware of its identification and importance in life.

Life, by its very nature, strives to be in balance. Problems become evident when it isn't. When any one part becomes burdensome, we fall over. It's as simple as that!

Think of your own life once again. Its excesses become destructive and the more the excess, the deeper the pit into which we fall. The descent is a seemingly endless spiral from which some of us desperately try to recover. If the struggle is successful, we continue on the path of life. If it isn't, we are doomed to misery.

From time to time we are apt to forget the words to the song of life. But that doesn't mean it's over. We can always hum, for a while, at least, but not forever. I might point out that life's music, also by its very nature, is almost always in balance. And it doesn't matter whether the song is sad or lively. If it's harmonious, and within a reasonable framework, chances are it's in balance. If it is discordant, then it can be the forerunner of an unhappy life. The challenge is to learn to sing the song of life and stay in tune with it.

Nothing exists by itself. Balance requires communication. It's the same thing as dancing. One partner usually leads, and the other follows. Both have the right to exist; the leading depends on the following and the following depends on the leading and both recognize that. The communication is the transfer of energy taking place between the two. The purpose is not superiority or inferiority of one or the other individual, but the flow between them.

Only in understanding and embracing this dance, can we understand each other. For me, the meaning of Balance is:

The power & respect for everything's nature.

Life is a very thin thread, stretched very far, connected in so many ways, a thin thread that can snap at any moment, a thread that relies solely on a million other things happening exactly as they do down to the very tiniest fraction of amillisecond. A very fragilebody, a soft mind. And a state of living that is in the hands of twenty degrees, anything below 90 Fahrenheit is death, anything above 110 Fahrenheit is death.

You actually live within 20 degrees. Balance

Notion of *Normal*?

EARTH without ART is E- - -H
How can my He(Art) wake the world?

THE DEFINITION OF NORMAL:
1. CONFORMING TO THE STANDARD OR THE COMMON TYPE; USUAL; NOT ABNORMAL; REGULAR; NATURAL.

2. SERVING TO ESTABLISH A STANDARD.

3. PSYCHOLOGY: APPROXIMATELY AVERAGE IN ANY PSYCHOLOGICAL TRAIT, AS INTELLIGENCE, PERSONALITY, OR EMOTIONAL ADJUSTMENT.

I pray that we are not normal! That we are anything but normal, standard, average, regular! "*Average intelligence, average personality*" – if that is normal, I will take the other side any day!

Someone says to me that I am not normal – I say "Thank you!"

I beat to a different drum – "Thank you!"

I'm different – "Thank you!"

What is normal? Getting a job in the city because it's safe and has benefits? Not being the first one to dance at a party? Not dancing and singing alone, for no other reason than expression and celebration? Having a mortgage?

Normal sounds like a prison.

We are addicted to normal, we are afraid to know life without it. But I promise you, when we start to strip away normal, chip and crack its veneer, there is such freedom, such power, such growth. That is where human potential and change lie, in your true self, the you who is anything but normal.

The Perfection problem?

"We come to love not by finding a perfect person, but by learning to see an imperfect person perfectly." — Sam Keen, To Love and Be Loved

I'm not perfect, and neither are you. Accept yourself fully—achievements, strengths, weaknesses, failures, flaws and all. You don't have to be perfect to realize your dreams, but you do need to be committed to personal growth. You can only begin that journey when you accept yourself completely for who you are.

Perfect doesn't exist, only LIFE exists: It's the bumps and lumps that make life memorable. Embrace the chaos. In Buddhism the first step to happiness is accepting, "That in this life there will be suffering" – Buddha.

The second rule – "all things will change, do not be attached"

Let go of your definition of seamless and tell yourself, perfect is boring.

Replace the old adage "Practice makes perfect," with this one, **Practice makes BETTER**:

It may not have been my piano teacher who said this for the first time, but she was the one who drilled it into my head. You can play the same piece over and over, practicing your whole life and still never play it exactly as it was meant to be performed.

I used to view that as a challenge, but as I've blossomed into an artist I see that as a fact. Even the person who wrote the music can't recreate the same thing over and over; only a machine can do that. No matter what you apply that to, whether it be an athletic event, a day at the office or an afternoon in the garden, it's true. You can work hard, practice, your whole life, but perfection isn't just about you. Circumstances change, weather shifts and people interfere. But if you're not trying to be perfect, just better than you were before, it is just about you and what you can do.

**~~Money~~. Paper.
You going to allow a piece of paper to stop you?**

"Anyone who lives within their means suffers from a lack of imagination." — Oscar Wilde

Money most of the time in today's society has a negative connotation, that doesn't mean it doesn't exist. I acknowledge its presence and it's capabilities for me to motivate, inspire, touch, and cause change within the world. I embrace that the world wants me to be my highest self, and to help me it will give me funds and opportunities in abundance to make my dreams come true to continue living life to its fullest.

I am not tied to it, but I know that it is drawn to me and I embrace that. Plus what I receive I will give back tenfold.

But I say again, its *paper*. That's all it is, nothing more.

BLOW IT UP!!!

"I don't want to make money, I just want to be wonderful." — Marilyn Monroe

Everything you though about it, change it, explode it, throw it all away

Paper – nothing more.
You can tear it, you can burn it, you can crumple it. It can be taken from you and not returned.

It can be multiplied and manufactured.
It's paper and it makes us mad. Tears at our minds. Makes us weak.
Changed the word money to love. There is enough love to go around. The more love you freely give away the more you will receive in return.
Changed its hold on us. Stopped chasing it and allowed it to come to us. Stopped living on its terms, but rather made it step up and support our terms. Paper cannot stop you. A weak and scared mind filled with worrisome thoughts can. We must change

our perspective. Fill our heart, minds, pockets, homes, with love, nothing but love, brimming with love.

Turn the word, "Money" into "**LOVE**"
There isn't a shortage of Love.
Love is in abundance. Enough to go around.
You can always afford to Love. We can always afford to Love more. Openly. Freely. Without restraints or conditions.
Money is a word, to describe a piece of paper. It only has as much power as we give it. Priorities and Perspective.
Like happiness, you'll never find it by forcing your will towards it, but it will land in your lap if you just are. **Love will come to you** if you don't search for it, need it, shape your life around it; it doesn't define you. It can't!

It is your right on this planet, in this life to be rich. To be wealthy.
The question is - Rich with what? Wealthy is what to you?

Does money have a hold on you? Are you living in fear that the pieces of paper might disappear?

We can survive without money; try surviveing without water, food, love, and a sense of purpose.

Free yourself. Live. Move forward. Live for the things you love and I guarantee you will reap the rewards tenfold – the abundance will come knocking down your door!

"Seven Deadly Sins Wealth without work Pleasure without conscience Science without humanity Knowledge without character Politics without principle Commerce without morality Worship without sacrifice." — Mahatma Gandhi

Saying "What if", "I wish" or "I hope":

"Never put off till tomorrow what may be done day after tomorrow just as well". — Mark Twain

Whenever you do this, you put yourself in a mindset where the situation is beyond your control. What you can do as an alternative is turn your wishes and hopes into goals. For example, don't say, "I wish my boss would give me flexible working hours."
Instead, set a goal that you're going to have a conversation with your boss within the next three days about establishing flexible working hours. When you set goals, you choose to focus on what you can do to improve your circumstances, which is very empowering.

What if your boss says No? You'll still be better off. You might start a conversation about flexible hours that other employees will be grateful for. Or you might find out where you stand with your employer in a way you didn't before. It's not always going to be about getting everything you want that instant, but an accumulation of positive change that you build upon in these moments. There might be a no and that's cool…

This freelancer right here, working actor can tell you – working independently in my own home office was an achievement made up of thousands of such tiny steps!

Saying, "I should" or "I can't."

Get your "but" out of your mouth and know that "Can't" means "Won't".

"Stop Shoulding on yourself" – Tony Robbins

Shoulds make the human mind sick. Throw should in the trash! Child shouldn't, car shouldn't, spouse shouldn't, boss shouldn't… accept reality, and all you can control is you.

When you say you "should" learn a new language, start writing a book, or go for a public speaking course, it's unlikely that you'll actually do it. Say, **"I choose to"** instead. This makes you realize that everything in life is a choice. You really do have the power to choose, and to turn your dreams into reality.

Still thinking of reasons why you shouldn't? There will always be plenty of them. Think of all the positive things that might happen if you take action today. Turn your *shoulds* into *coulds*. Are you ready to stop shoulding and start **doing?**

Comparing Yourself to Others:

Create don't compete
Create together

No more comparing us to others, there will always be people out there who are better looking, smarter and more capable than you. But you're not trying to achieve their dreams; you're trying to achieve yours. Think about the characteristics that make you special and unique, and about how you can use them to accomplish your dream.

Our school system/life: We study and learn in order to get ahead;
How about we study and learn because it's FUN.

We are confined only by the walls we have built around ourselves.

"Reality is merely an illusion, albeit a very persistent one" – Albert Einstein

We can be someone who is just another thing, who does things that don't really matter, or we can know, "we exist, we matter!"
Every breath matters, every step is huge. We can make a difference, we'll succeed, there is no other way.

Making Excuses:

We are now excusing ourselves from the excuses
As to why we are not joyful
Healthy
Happy.
We now give up all excuses as to why we can't be
Brilliant
Happy
Creative
Grateful.
Excuses be gone
Excuses be gone
Excuses are gone.
We are excusing ourselves from excuses
The excuse can be quicksand, a sinkhole
Or if examined properly it becomes a way in.
To all the things we truly are, deserve, and are meant to have.
Who am I going to be without my excuses?
The cosmos. The embodiment of strength. My true, unmatched self.

Perceiving Time Poverty vs. Time Affluence:

"I'm the one that's got to die when it's time for me to die, so let me live my life the way I want to." — Jimi Hendrix

Dead Lines vs. Life Lines
I got-to vs. I get-to

You must get there or you die or the things we want to do, they inspire us, they fill us with inspiration, they give us life.
Living time as opposed to killing time.

You have time.

"I find television very educating. Every time somebody turns on the set, I go into the other room and read a book."
— Groucho Marx

Really? Do you make time to watch your favorite TV show? Do you make time to update your Facebook status? Do you make time to eat? We all make time for the things that are important to us. If you find yourself saying you "don't have time" to do something you know you ought to, you need to reorder your priorities.

Next time someone says A.S.A.P. – ALWAYS SAY A PRAYER. Pray to anything, pray to pray, and pray to practice.

The Question of Luck:

Luck

I don't believe in luck or that things happen by chance.

I come from the school of thought: "Ask and you shall receive"

Now that doesn't mean it will be handed down to you from God in a glowing orb and shining beam of light with an orchestra of angels playing harps.

How I see it: Is that you ask and then prepare yourself to build the house one brick at a time. You are prepared to fall and take wrong turns, because it's all about the journey – *We can know where we're going, where we'll end up, but we can't possibly know how we're going to get there.*

The fact is too many blessings have happened which have kept me out of harms way; where the speeding ticket made me 25 minutes late, and only being that late did I run into someone by "chance" who made me kiss the ground for that speeding ticket.

I also know that having that much Faith is trying, and a lot of work; to accept all of it as good, as a part of the journey. To feel like you are not in control sometimes sucks. But when you allow yourself to be in that state, more and more, then the lack of control feeling becomes more and more of an afterthought, you begin seeing, smelling, and feeling the world differently.

Just keep living, keep thinking big. Positive energy and a focused mind, and be prepared to WORK. WORK HARD.

Stop labeling things as good and bad, or lucky and unlucky. It's all a part of the journey, we just have to surrender a little bit of our own will and allow the universe to take some of the weight.

Luck isn't just about being at the right place at the right time, but also about being open to and ready for new opportunities. As Richard Wiseman's ten-year study has shown:

Lucky people generate good fortune via four basic principles. They are skilled at creating and noticing chance opportunities, make lucky decisions by listening to their intuition, create self-fulfilling prophesies via positive expectations, and adopt a

resilient attitude that transforms bad luck into good.

Are you a lucky or unlucky person? Or, to put it more precisely, are you prepared to be lucky?

3. WORK YOUR BUILDING BLOCKS:

You've accepted the landscape; you're dodging the traps, now you're ready to strengthen the building blocks of your new life.

Honesty

"If you do not tell the truth about yourself you cannot tell it about other people." — Virginia Woolf

Enhance your likelihood of success (speak your truth).
Don't react, respond.

When the Buddha returned to his son after 9 years of searching, he gave his 7-year-old son Rahula one lecture, it was a *big* lecture but I'm going to summarize it in two paragraphs:

A) Never tell a lie. Anyone who can tell you the slightest of lies is also capable of any evil. We've seen this repeatedly in the financial world.

B) For every physical, verbal, emotional, and mental action you take, FOCUS before, during, and after to make sure nobody is getting hurt.

That's it. Beautiful. It's all you need to live a good life.

Strength

"The weak can never forgive. Forgiveness is the attribute of the strong." — Mahatma Gandhi

A flowers beauty comes form the fact that it is not strong.
The roots are strong, but the flower not so much.
It opens its petals to welcome the sun.
Dances with the wind, the rain, and the sun and by evening the petals are falling off.

*"All that is gold does not glitter,
not all those who wander are lost;
the old that is strong does not wither,
Deep roots are not reached by the frost.*

*From the ashes a fire shall be woken,
A light from the shadows shall spring;
Renewed shall be blade that was broken,
The crownless again shall be king."*
— J.R.R. Tolkien, The Fellowship of the Ring

The real F words – Forgiveness & Freedom

"Always forgive your enemies; nothing annoys them so much." — Oscar Wilde

Add an N to "Forgive" and it is done.

Without forgiveness there is no freedom. This FREEDOM we are always talking about is your birthright.
Freedom from belief systems, of who you think you are, what you think you should be, and how you should spend your days.
Freedom from resentment and toxicity. Freedom from envy.
Freedom. We know this. We know that we are more than these experiences, more than these emotions, more than this body- this is the part that I call FREEDOM, this knowing, living from our gut, hearing the call, higher purpose, higher power (whatever words work for you).
Freedom from the bondage of our own perception, freedom from what the mind tells the brains to do, synapses from the body, and the mind changes it – delete that, add that, change that so you can stay in your paradigm, stay in your place so that we don't see the divine! …

"Woah is me, to see what I see, see what I see" – *Hamlet*

The freedom to: Express yourself, to embody joy, to have Heaven on Earth, to wake up.
Everything is asking you: *"Won't you please see me correctly so I can be free? Won't you get out of the way? Set me free."*
As long as we are bound to the old issues weighing us down, we can't truly be free.

That's where we must learn to forgive. Freedom comes from Forgiveness – forgiveness is not a feeling, it's a *declaration*, it's an act you take over and over again, its stand you take over and over again.

Either no one deserves forgiveness or everyone deserves forgiveness.

Forgiveness is realizing that what you think your brother did to you never happened at all

Your continued resentment (to others or the self) is not going to inspire change. Most people cannot self-correct, they self-reflect, they deflect when they feel like they have to defend themselves.
When we forgive it doesn't mean we are inviting them or these old habits back into our lives… It doesn't mean we are asking them back into our life… *"I forgive you and we are not going to do lunch"*…
When we forgive ourselves: *"I forgive that wrong in me and I am not inviting it back into my life."*

This freedom is ours, ours to manifest, create, work for, and uncover. When you dream you don't wake up from a bad dream and blame the guy next to you... So why do we do it in this dream called life?

Forgive, allow, accept, love, move forward and be free!

Freedom:

"Lock up your libraries if you like; but there is no gate, no lock, no bolt that you can set upon the freedom of my mind." — Virginia Woolf, A Room of One's Own

Freedom is not like other phenomena. It's closer to "being" than it is to some "thing." It has nothing to do with options. It requires dimensionality—if we try to move freedom through a world of limited possibility, it can never show up as itself, it's always distorted as something else. Freedom doesn't live in a temporality like past, present, and future—it doesn't stop, in the same way that "number" doesn't stop giving numbers or that art is not repeating, in a new way, the past. There's nothing pulling one way or the other, there is just this awesome freedom. Freedom is about choosing—it's about the profoundly human ability to create.

We commonly think of freedom as "freedom from," "freedom of," or "freedom to" do or be something, or as the ability to define alternatives and select among them. But freedom far exceeds anything on that spectrum—it's being able to redefine ourselves and reality at large, generating a whole new sets of possibilities. History is punctuated by such redefinitions—creative acts that open new worlds. In this sense, we can call creative acts the edge of freedom—the faculty by which, down through history, we have redefined our world and ourselves.

We are attracted to **Freedom**. I have never really been attracted to danger, but freedom, yes! And happiness, music, art, healthy eating, healthy living, spirituality, meditation, diet and exercise, releasing oneself from old habits, and releasing oneself from negative ways of thinking seemed the conduit for such freedom.

Giving & Receiving

See & Sea are spelt differently, sound exactly the same, one is to see, like I'm looking at you, I see you — but we all know just because you're being looked at doesn't mean you've been seen. The other is to bathe, I bathe in the Sea, I bathe in you, because when I'm not looking at you, I'm seeing you, and when I see you I bathe in you.

When Japanese monks carry out their traditional alms rounds, their faces are partly hidden under their wide straw hats, which also prevent them from seeing the faces of those giving to them. "No giver, no receiver", no strings attached. In our culture, we're accepting the challenge of asking, giving, and receiving — face to face. Sometimes you ask, and I give. Sometimes I ask, and you give. And always we're receiving, life endlessly giving, and moment after moment.

The highest gift of all, says the Buddha, is the gift of Dharma, the mindfulness teachings of wisdom and compassion. This gift has the power to change a life. When we receive this gift and practice together, it is inevitable: that our meanness becomes com passionate, our restlessness, peaceful, our selfishness becomes generous and our stubbornness, forgiving.

This is freedom. This is happiness.

All roads have led to here and we know how lucky we are to walk them day in and day out. Here at Lifestyle Dezine this is one of our ways of sharing unconditionally.

This is to us is the importance of living — "No giver, no receiver", no strings attached. In our culture, we're accepting the challenge of asking, giving, and receiving — face to face.

Sometimes you ask, and I give. Sometimes I ask, and you give. And always we're receiving, life endlessly giving, and moment after moment.

Curiosity & Questions

"I am the empty void. It counters the big bang. It all starts with nothing-ness." - Buddha

In alchemy (The ability to turn nothing into something, coal into gold), mystery & magic are the final ingredients.

Questions are good, we need to allow ourselves to

be ignorant, the questions make us lean forward, it keeps us going... you may find the answer, you may ask the question again, the answer changes, you can never step in the same river twice.

Who am I? What is my question?
I want to make a difference in the world?
How do I wake up the world?
How do I show every person that they matter?
How do I find? Become? And cultivate complete freedom?

Curiosity is beautiful / Loss is Joy.
We enjoy the curious vs. the know it all.
The artist vs. the politician.
It's about knowing what you don't know.
The wise man knew he knew nothing at all.
Intellect alone will not save you.

Peace in Uncertainty

Curiosity and questions will teach you to live at peace in uncertainty. And our world is uncertain, so that's a good thing.

Uncertainty is an uncomfortable place. Certainty is an absurd place.

> *"One person's craziness is another person's reality." — Tim Burton*

We don't know enough to be atheist - 90% of the known universe is Dark Matter - that's a lot to sweep under the rug.

We know enough to not believe in a single thing - the universe was possibly thrown up by a giant white monster, possibly not, possibly given to us by two naked people, a talking reptile, and dirty produce, possibly not.

Why don't we celebrate possibility and praise uncertainty?

I'm not going to live frustrated because I am uncomfortable. I'm not going to be upset because things are not happening on my timetable. I'm not going to fight against everything that I don't like.

Got-to into Get-to

I get to
Not got to

Turn got-to
Into **get**-to

I get to go into the office. I get to live today. I get to wake up early. I get to live my life to its fullest. I get to pray. I get to meditate. I get to read. Play. I get to love

Yes to You

A "no" to someone can be a "yes" to you (and you deserve a yes) You are So(ul) Amazing.

Many people find it impossible to say "no" to requests and opportunities, even ones that aren't in line with their values and goals. If you say, "yes" to everyone, you're effectively settling for good, when what you really want is great. The path of greatness is the path of intentional abandonment of everything good, in pursuit of only the best. Think carefully before agreeing to any request. "You can please all of the people some of the time, and some of the people all of the time, but you can't please all of the people all of the time." Your dreams are personal. You're not pursuing them to garner applause from the people around you or from society. Don't make the mistake of trying to make everyone happy, because that's impossible. So don't even try.

NOW FLY:

"Happiness is the consequence of personal effort. You fight for it, strive for it, insist upon it, and sometimes even travel around the world looking for it. You have to participate relentlessly in the manifestations of your own blessings. And once you have achieved a state of happiness, you must never become lax about maintaining it. You must make a mighty effort to keep swimming upward into that happiness forever, to stay afloat on top of it." – Elizabeth Gilbert

No longer waiting, you have become.

"Spiritus," the Latin origin of the word "spirit", literally means "breath"… To feel spirit is to breathe, to breathe is to be filled with spirit. Allow the breath to breathe you!
It's a tiny shift on the computer key to move my heart's desire from "nowhere to be found" to "now here to be found."

Will you believe me when I tell you there's kindness in your heart? That all things are here to serve you? That what you want wants to be with you, you just have to say yes? That all your needs are met?

You are here in this world because you couldn't tolerate any other place.

The one eyed man is king in the land of the blind. Lets open our eyes. Lets wake up. Lets be Queens and Kings.

Whatever you can do, begin it. Boldness has magic, power, and love within it.

Science fiction writer Arthur C. Clarke wrote: *A wise man once said that all human activity is a form of play. And the highest form of play is the search for Truth, Beauty and Love. What more is needed? Should there be a 'meaning' as well, that will be a bonus?*
If we waste time looking for life's meaning, we may have no time to live — or to play.

"Those who danced were thought to be quite insane by those who could not hear the music."
–Angela Monet

So…
What will the world do when you let your wings out? When you define and create your own truths. Live your life. Create your freedom. When you become your superhuman self?

When you break out from the crowd?

Lets find out!

I know that there will be times when you will have to stand and speak. Those who are for you, will stand beside you and say "thank you, thank you, thank you! Because your freedom is my freedom! Thank you."

And some will leave you, your power, your truth will frighten them, they will back away, running back to normal, a world without wings, a sleeping world.

I can no longer be small. I can no longer sit back. Like the 14-year-old girl who spoke up against the Taliban because she refused to be silenced. **I ask you to join me in letting *your* wings out!**

To be anything but normal.

Go out there and Paint your World.

You. The artist, the dreamer, the beautiful body and soul.

You are inspiration to the world around you.

You are shedding inspiration, love, light, peace, compassion, and joy with all you encounter…

Or, you're shedding grime, sorrow, despair, guilt, attachment, jealousy, and envy to name a few.

We are watching, what are you giving?

We are open, what are you sharing?

You are a painter: The words you speak, the thoughts you think, and the love you give, they all color this world.

What are we sharing? What are we giving? How can we, how are we making it possible to allow f**lowers to grow from the rubbl**e?

Perspective.

Being a leader, means standing for truth. If we breathe we matter, we lead, we leave things behind, if you're reading this book, you know this, you know your worth…

"What lies behind us and what lies before us are tiny matters compared to what lies within us."
– Ralph Waldo Emerson

"A leader is really the symbolic soul of group consciousness." – Deepak Chopra

A real leader unlocks not only his or her own potential but also the potential of everyone on the planet. He or she harnesses the evolutionary impulse of the universe for greater good, truth, harmony, justice, and equality. Spiritual leadership is the call to rectify all of the problems that plague humanity right now, whether it's radical poverty or social injustice or war or conflict or ecological devastation—and not at the level at which they were created but from this deeper level where we cannot help but bring light where there is darkness.

A True leader isn't afraid to step out and be seen. They encourage it, welcome it with open arms, they say, "I am awake to the ultimate reality and to the deepest truth of who we all really are, and I'm willing to stand for that in all the imperfection of my evolving humanity."

These are the leaders the world needs now. It's all too easy to sit back, observe what the problems are, and fall into a state of despair or cynicism. It takes **courage** to step forward and begin to take responsibility for the solution in our own ways. Our lives making a significant difference depends on two things: how wholeheartedly and with how much commitment are we willing to do all the things our heart beckons us to do.

One of the best ways to make you happy is to make someone else happy.
One of the best ways to make someone else happy is to be happy yourself.
Happy people make people happy. Making people happy makes people happy.

We are committing to our growth.

I am committed to myself so that I can feel good in my skin, so that I can shine from within. I'm committed to my body. I'm committed to my mind. I'm committed to knowing thyself. I am committed to excellence.

"So therefore I dedicate myself to myself, to my art, my sleep, my dreams, my labors, my sufferance, my loneliness, my unique madness, my endless absorption and hunger- because I cannot dedicate myself to any fellow being." - **Jack Kerouac**

Think left and think right and think low and think high. Oh, the thinks you can think up if only you try!
~Dr. Seuss

By the time you finish your dictionary, it'll be out of date. **Time to start again.**

THIS IS YOUR LIFE, your dreams, your words, your stories, your blood, your scars, your breath, and your sweat. All of it is yours.

"Enthusiasm" comes from the two little Greek words en and theos- "Enthusiasm" literally means: "God within" Or "Possessed by a God". In every second be enthusiastic for the many gifts and blessings you have.

What story will you write? What words will you use as you write yourself a masterpiece?

We are shaped by our thoughts; **we become what we think**. *When the mind is pure, joy follows like a shadow that never leaves.* **~Buddha**

There's a great division coming about on this planet. There are going to be a lot of people who will die because they just don't know how to live. They don't know what life's about, they don't know how to give, how to love - nor do they want to.

And those who are beautiful enough - I don't mean physically but something beyond that - they will have the chance to learn how to fly, to be beautiful, to rise above the level of the normal human - to be superior beings first and eventually gods and goddesses.

www.ingramcontent.com/pod-product-compliance
Lightning Source LLC
Chambersburg PA
CBHW041522090426
42737CB00037B/11